What a sneakily brilliant thing! In *Sma...*
rhythms of life unravel, the threat and th...
absurd and transcendent. The images ar...
The speaker addresses us like a fav...
endlessly inquisitive. Georgieva diagnos...
but fleetingly redeeming, excavating fragile moments of beauty with a g...
touch and mordant wit.

— Vanessa Kisuule

In these brilliantly sly poems of displacement and theft, language circulates in
surreptitious and uncanny ways. Georgieva renders the riches of experience
with unsparing clarity, but the particles and objects of these poems somehow
slip, as in dreams, out of the reader's grasp. Things that should be most securely
personal — hands, hairs, memories, a familiar song — are lost or stolen away.
"Quickly we learn / of impermanence", the way the world changes even as
the body is caught in moments of stasis. These poems give us the world on a
knife-edge, waiting "for what the mind will do next" — a place of discomfort
articulated in all its strangeness, with mordant and rueful humour.

— James Wilkes

'The Details Here Are Not Important' is the title of one of the opening poems
of Yanita Georgieva's electric and witty debut pamphlet *Small Undetectable
Thefts* goes and yet they really are. Her expertly curated images — a cracked
pot / of blue jasmine, the wilt / of an abandoned / tulip, the neighbours /
rooting for us in their nightgowns, a gambler's / insatiable tongue — are the
existential signposts in this sweeping, film-noirish narrative which reads in
places like a feverous hybrid of Matthew Sweeney's alternative realism and
the sweet, off-kilter ingenuity of Selima Hill.

Georgieva lures us into this world and leads us in a search for answers
with the assistance of narrators who carry the weight of cities on their
shoulders, narrowly avoiding disaster, gripping onto the wheels of wayward
cars in a perpetual game of hide and seek with all the beauty just out of
reach, in the darkness of the margins. Her poetry feels like the sharp cusp of
desire and the sensation of a new season in a strange country. Through this
small, brave collection Georgieva communicates that there are some things
too painful to admit or to face head on and offers us instead small flashes of
light to illuminate the drab monotony of modern life.

Granting us the gift of the glimpse, *Small Undetectable Thefts* combines
the dream-like with the banal and tutors us in the sparkling art of the
mundane – through the washer, the spin cycle, or the ripe perfection of a
lime cut into wedges she explores the parameters of intimacy and memory.
Though as she writes in 'same old' that *we're too precious with endings,* by the
close of this stellar pamphlet we feel schooled in the aesthetics of dread,
the mysteries of faulty appliances, our stubborn, unknowable bodies, and the
quiet devastating power of the unarticulated.

— Lucy Holme

SMALL UNDETECTABLE THEFTS

Yanita Georgieva is a poet and journalist. She was born in Bulgaria, raised in Lebanon, and currently lives in England. She is a recipient of the Out-Spoken Prize for Page Poetry and a member of the Southbank New Poets Collective and the London Library Emerging Writers. You can find her work in *The London Magazine, Poetry Wales, bath magg*, and elsewhere.

ISBN: 978-1-916938-08-3

Cover designed by Aaron Kent

Edited and Typeset by Aaron Kent

Broken Sleep Books Ltd
PO BOX 102
Llandysul
SA44 9BG

CONTENTS

Small Undetectable Thefts

Yanita Georgieva

Broken Sleep Books

I SWEAR I KNEW NOTHING

No good jokes, no secrets,
no presidents' names,
not what Americans meant
when they said IN THE NAME
OF DEMOCRACY or why there were sheep
hanging upside down in the garage,
not silence, not outrage, not the men
shouting NICE JEANS at me from their cars,
not the number of annual burglaries
in five neighbouring postcodes or words
like postcode, hand job, duck confit,
in a simulated crash the dummy is never
a woman and I didn't know that
either, not yoga or burnout or the thrill
of crossing a small violet line.
Three men climbed on top of a yacht
and waltzed into our apartment.
We couldn't figure out what they'd stolen
but we knew we wanted it back.

THAT WAR, LIKE ANY OTHER WAR

We fled in an old Mercedes,
its door handles held together with tape.
The news made its way through in fragments
and I didn't understand the word
the grownups were trading
like an old, damaged bill.
Traffic was killer but the kids were ecstatic,
having been granted the day off to play
Smackdown; God of War. I was a coward, even then.
Spent the day in the attic wiping dust off our bags
with a wet cloth. From the balcony, we watched
the prime minister's coffin float through buildings
from one end of Liberty Street to the other. *We're leaving*,
said my mother, for the first but not the last time.

CIVIL SERVICE

I worry my best
work is not
so much the dog

running behind me
with a stick in its mouth
but the rat

placed gently on some
unsuspecting neighbour's porch
and left to rot

into spring; nothing
worth remembering
needs writing down

I read that in the paper then forgot another
birthday playdate and the uncapped
p in president as in one president

has announced a state
of emergency not
President So And So believes this particular

emergency is necessary
for the state I believe
the thought arrives after the feeling

I should have been
listening
closely

to the fizz of this or that
small metal object
breaking the greengrocer's windows

instead I was busy thinking
how nice it must be
not to carry fear like a pigeon

FOR ONE BRIEF MOMENT

Time spilled out
like pennies on kitchen tiles.

I imagined the neighbours
rooting for us in their nightgowns:

two kids catching a moment
and stretching it wide.

When we couldn't be alone,
we stood like red deer on the stairwell

listening for coughs, the threat
of an approaching lift.

Then our hands felt funny in the dark.

I remember thinking:
it will never be like this again –

not that it was beautiful,
but that we stole the night back.

That I held him, in the end.
It's easy now. Nobody cares what I do

with my body.
I could kiss him in so many rooms.

THE DEVIL IS BOWLING AGAIN

The fear – I don't miss it
though sometimes I wonder if it made me better
at listening, attentive not just to the tide
but the foam. I loved the world most
when it wanted to kill me. Now I catch a fox
licking the yolk off an eggshell and think
how much damage can it do?
Running through Waterloo station
on the phone to my sister, she says
it sounds like there's a problem there –
and I worry I can't hear it
anymore – worry I won't catch
the low screech of the dryer right before
it sets the flat ablaze. I'm trying to unhook myself
from the things I cannot change.
It's not about forgetting but deciding
what you cannot do without.

THINK ABOUT IT

The only good day of the week is Saturday.
The best use of your time is swimming.

The purest way to feel desire is to pluck it
fat and salty off the highest branch
and watch another mouth get to it first.

I like my freedom as much as the next guy,
but I want it to tickle my head and my feet at the same time.

When I first wet my hands with it,
I was scared of the streaks it left in the sink.
Now I want it buffet-style. Give me more

so I can watch the fruit flies circling its body
like a shrine. I would rather let it spoil
than go back to the way it was, the burning lack of it,

how we licked what we could off its surface
in small undetectable thefts
and called ourselves lucky.

Until it was gone.
Until there was none of it left.

SO, YOU LEAVE BEIRUT

Stick on your shoulder
and a small, knotted sheet.
You pass a row of burning tires
and because you are becoming
a virtuous person, you put them out
with your pointer and thumb.
You move into a flat with bed bugs
and a delicate mosaic sink,
learn how to dress for the job and develop
a terrible accent. You double your hours of service
to the land of choice –
which, not unlike the pot of gold
rumoured to be buried deep in the ravine,
no one tells you how to spend.
You come to the end
of a long shift. It is time
to make peace with your father.
When you call, he says:
this is a bad time.

IT IS WITH GREAT SADNESS

my life opened its mouth   and there was a forest
white button-ups hung   from the branches   like flags
the sun appeared briefly, as if to check   on its children
I am a child   I said to the sun
in one dream   I am armed   with a matchbox
I burn it all down   and in the burning   find something
like truth   at parties the bankers keep telling me   man
only needs silence   a deer   in the bushes
we seem to be looking   at different   trees
I left flowers in the place   where it happened   as if
to say something but   I couldn't say   anything

CONFESSION

I didn't cry enough the night I found out.
Sat there in the dark

and put food in my mouth.
I kept showing up to his flat

even after they had cleared it of his stuff.
Did my job. Sold a flight to Dubai.

I watched two men dump his mattress
in the woods and said nothing, didn't cry there,

not even in the nice lady's office
when I asked how it happened and she answered

before I could stop her. I wish I'd held the word
in mid-air for a moment or two.

It's selfish, a man writes in the Times, to say *I*
in a poem. To take out the bins in his absence.

In dreams, he wears a cream jumper
and acts unlike himself.

ITALIANISE THIS

The word for disaster I love most is *casino,*
implying ruin will come with a heap of white tokens
and drinks on the house. *They pay you to stay here,*
say the gamblers at the lunch buffet, like how at the wake
they kept bringing out figs wrapped in bacon to keep us
happy, fed. I have left so much of the past for the dogs
to chew like a slipper. The peonies drop all their leaves
at once in a heap, and I can't bear to empty the vases
of their headless stems. Once you've fished a blackbird
limp out of the well, you learn what it means to go on
in an absence. I, too, have looked at the water
flashing bright and unruly, and wondered.
It takes strength to pull the dead thing out
though it offers no resistance.

SAME OLD

I saw it once through a hole in the wall
and even then, I wasn't really looking.
Now the memory is odd in its movement.
I can't put my hands on its body
and name what I'm touching, torso, earlobe,
rounded back, so what if it happened?
When he died, I was sure I'd never have the pleasure
of a fresh thought, locked as I was
in the screening of his life, and even that ended.
One morning on the bus to work, I found myself
picturing a Swedish summer. Buttered bread.
Time unbuckled me, without warning.
The past is a beautiful friend
with whom I feel daft and unlikeable.
We are here at this party.
Where do I put down what happened?
What do I do with my hands?

THE DETAILS HERE ARE NOT IMPORTANT

maybe there was
a washing machine
on the roof

a cracked pot
of blue jasmine
teetering over
the parapet

I was there
with my big
mouth
pulling up
my wet skirt

the rain came
in ladles which
is not important now

I see them all
the things I should have done

locked the roof garden
twisted and pulled out
each tooth like a tick
yelled about women
and cockpits and pecking

for worms
I should have
said something
better but
if you are wondering
if I waited

                    yes,

with the wilt
of an abandoned
tulip I waited
and waited
to be plucked out
of the mulch

for a swamp mouth
to open and call me
a good green thing
worthy of light

I AM LEARNING TO COMMIT

The way an acorn dives
into a parking lot

or a birch leaf sticks it out
until the lurid end

out of inertia, valour, what
I couldn't tell you.

Someone has to do it –

part with their hairline,
pick out a stroller,

and boil the tomatoes
lest they all go to waste.

For every dribbling baby, there is a mother
looking intently, translating to speech.

How can I summon her here?
Even at my own dissection,

I wouldn't be certain what everything is.
I think I know what I want but

I'm waiting, I keep telling my lover,
for one of our friends to try it out first.

POSH SALAD

Since it's just us, we can look at this egg and call it a baby. One year my body was serving a purpose (thick octopus costume) then another (sea-slicked revenge suit) now I just Google hip pain a lot. I don't know how I'd care for a tadpole, but that feels important. What would I do with an electric blue jellyfish, its wet jewelled tentacles splayed in my palm? Everyone says *you'll know what to do*, like a slippery omen from the ocean's mouth. Every minute with children feels like a test. What if they think I don't get it? What if after all those piercing critiques of my mother, I do everything wrong? Every salt cliff picking its skin is an invitation to jump. Some nights I wake up thinking I've ruined my life. It's always the same dream: two sweaty hands on the wheel of a car I can't drive.

OUR PLACE

The washer is refusing to drain. A jar of miso cracked the stovetop. The oak floors warped and soaked up all our neighbours' baths, and just last week, we shivered in the shower, pouring kettle water on our feet. But we are determined. Every day we learn to fix things with our hands. First, we warm our legs without a working boiler. Then, we learn to ease the front door off its hinges, let its weight lean into one of us while the other lifts it open. Tonight, we're squatting in the kitchen, passing trays of murky water back and forth like an elaborate machine. Soon enough, the washer's drum stops leaking, and we pull the filter out to find the culprit. We splash down on the wet tiles, watch the animal we tamed and nursed ease back into its body. It's beautiful – the washer, the spin cycle, the kitchen you called me from last year saying, *I can picture you here, cutting a lime into wedges.*

HOW WE LOSE IT

Shedding starts at the head.
That's how snakes do it.

A cicada's less patient,
leaping fast
out of its casing.

Crabs do it too
backing out slowly, leaving
a ghost shell, an outline in chalk.

I'm in a forest
littered with past lives,
the hollow still clinging
to grass.

In the river, a figure's
white silhouette
discarded like wedding lace.

Tell me. Wouldn't you do it?

Step out of your body
and run?

IT'S NEW BECAUSE IT'S DIFFERENT

When I start to lose my hair
        I see it everywhere:

milky petals falling from a branch,
        a handful of grass

leaving an imprint of itself, two coins
        growing rounder in my palm.

I become so good at counting
        losses. One website says

a hundred wet hairs in the shower
        is normal; I pretend I haven't seen

the other fifty. The first time it happened,
        I was in preschool, wearing a bandana

and a lime green suit. The next, we were so close
        to shaving it off, when

out of nowhere, peach fuzz sprouted
        on the edges of a small moon. This time

we are standing by the draughty window
        with the good light. I pull my hair back

from the new spot, like a curtain drawn
       before the show. He brings out

the tape measure, pressing cool hard plastic
       to my skin. *It hasn't grown,*

he tells me. *But it's starting to look*
       like a bird.

IN THE ABSENCE OF

Without the proper attention, a peace lily will lower its blades
looking for water. Without delicate wisps framing the face,
a skull is a skull, no softness about it. Without softness,
who knows what a woman might do. Without touch,
my hands dried out in the sun. Without consent,
I was flung from one end to another and swung.
Without the family duvet, which I left at
the airport. Without words weighing
down pockets. Later, without words.
Without room to learn or become.
Without room. Without country,
when told to fuck off back
to my country. For years,
without voice. For years,
without body. Then
finally a body
w i t h o u t

ACKNOWLEDGEMENTS

Thank you to the incredible writers who helped inspire, shape, and polish the poems in this book, especially Alana Chase, Georgia Luckhurst, Kitty Hawkins, James Wilkes, Alia Kobuszko, Jack Wright, Sean Borodale, Lavinia Greenlaw, Will Harris, Vanessa Kissuule, Sophie Ransby, and the Southbank New Poets Collective.

Thank you to the Dreamboat Collective poets – Jessica Barrie, Osama Brosh, Temenuzhka Marinova, and John Stubbins – without whom these poems would not exist.

Thank you to Aaron, Charlie, and the Broken Sleep team for taking a chance on this book. Thank you to the editors at bath magg, Northern Gravy, The Mechanics' Institute Review, Bahr Magazine, and The North for publishing earlier versions of some of these poems.

Thank you, Beirut. Thank you, Mira, Rami, mum, and my wonderful family. And thank you Sam and Gene, for everything.

LAY OUT YOUR UNREST

9 781916 938083